Eating Right

Jenny Reznick

Sadlier-Oxford
A Division of William H. Sadlier, Inc.

Contents

The Bread and
  Grain Group 6

The Vegetable Group ... 8

The Fruit Group 10

The Milk Group 12

The Meat and
  Fish Group 14

The Eating Right
  Pyramid 16

My Health Project 19

Index 20

Meet Lin and Mac. They know that eating right means choosing foods from five important food groups.

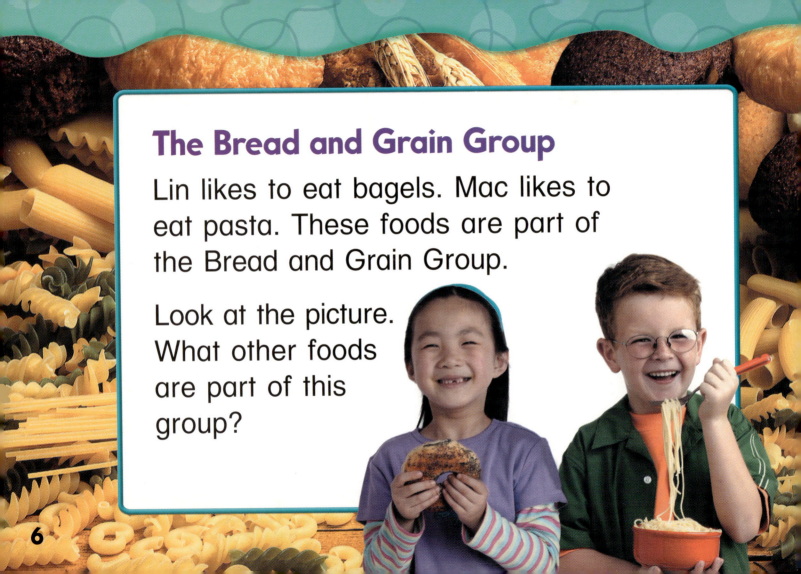

The Bread and Grain Group

Lin likes to eat bagels. Mac likes to eat pasta. These foods are part of the Bread and Grain Group.

Look at the picture. What other foods are part of this group?

The Vegetable Group

Lin and Mac both like to munch on carrots. They like the crunchy sound carrots make. Carrots are part of the Vegetable Group.

What other foods are part of the Vegetable Group?

The Fruit Group

Lin likes to eat apples. Mac likes to eat bananas. These foods are part of the Fruit Group.

What other fruits can you name?

The Milk Group

Lin and Mac like milk. Lin drinks a glass of milk. Mac pours some on his cereal.

Milk is part of the Milk Group. Cheese and yogurt are, too. Can you guess why?

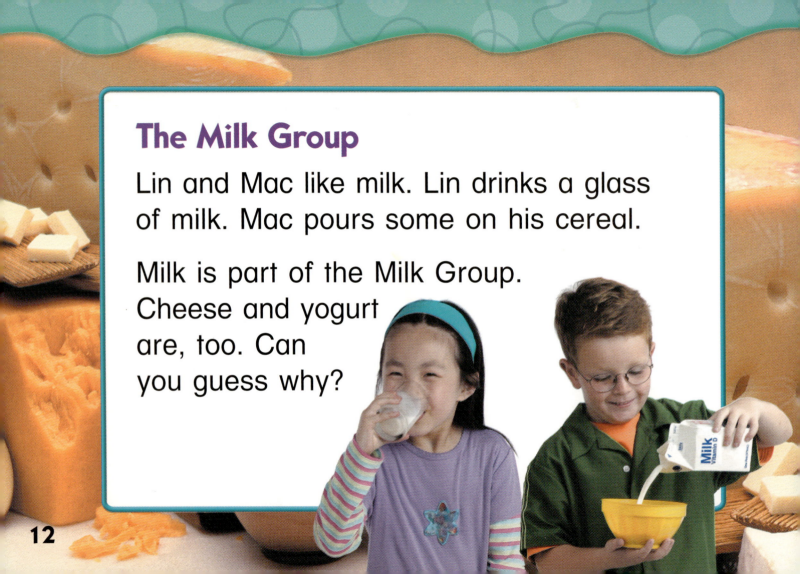

The Meat and Fish Group

Lin likes to eat chicken. Mac likes to eat tuna. These foods are part of the Meat and Fish Group.

Nuts, dried beans, and eggs are also part of this group. What food from this group do you like best?

The Eating Right Pyramid

Look at this chart. It shows how many servings a day to eat from each food group.

Fats and Sweets
Eat less

Milk Group
2–3 servings

Meat and Fish Group
2–3 servings

Vegetable Group
3–5 servings

Fruit Group
2–4 servings

Bread and Grain Group
6–11 servings

Here's a snack that has foods from three food groups. Can you name the groups?

Eating Right Snack

What You Need:

 blueberries   granola   yogurt

1. Put a layer of granola in a tall glass.
2. Add some yogurt.
3. Add some blueberries.
4. Add more layers.

At snacktime or mealtime, be like Lin and Mac. Choose foods from the five food groups and you'll be eating right!

My Health Project

Make and Match Food Cards

What You Need:

5 cards

crayons

glue

scissors

magazines

What You Do:

1. Think about the five food groups. Draw or glue a picture of a food from a different group on each card.
2. Put your cards with a partner's.
3. Use the cards to play Concentration. Match foods from the same group.

Index

apples, 10

bagels, 6

bananas, 10

blueberries, 17

Bread and Grain Group, 6–7, 16

carrots, 8

cheese, 12

chicken, 14

dried beans, 14

Eating Right Pyramid, 16–17

eggs, 14

food groups, 5, 16, 17, 18

Fruit Group, 10–11, 16

granola, 17

Meat and Fish Group, 14–15, 16

Milk Group, 12–13, 16

milk, 12

nuts, 14

pasta, 6

snack, 17

tuna, 14

Vegetable Group, 8–9, 16

yogurt, 12, 17